THE DIMENSIONS OF SUCCESS

THE DIMENSIONS

OF SUCCESS

CREATING SUCCESS ONE DIMENSION AT A TIME

JAMIE ADAMCHUK

THE DIMENSIONS OF SUCCESS
CREATING SUCCESS ONE DIMENSION AT A TIME

© 2017 **JAMIE ADAMCHUK**

ISBN 978-0-9952162-1-1 paperback
ISBN 978-0-9952162-2-8 eBook

A portion of the profits from the sale of this book will be donated to the JASH Foundation, in support of providing free education for separated and divorcing parents.

DEDICATION

To Steffany Haynes, my beautiful wife, my partner in crime and my soulmate, you are the force that shaped me into the man I have become, and without you, none of this would have been possible. There's no way I could ever thank you enough for your constant dedication to fueling my passion for making a difference in so many people's lives. I love you, baby.

To all my friends and teachers along the path of my life – far too many to name, who have challenged me to grow well beyond anything I could have ever dreamed. So many of you have had such a profound impact on me, and because of that, I'll be forever grateful.

And to my son Brandon, it's through you that I've been given the gift of seeing the world through a new set of eyes. You continually show me what's possible and how to become an even better father, empowering me to take these new skills and make an even bigger difference in the world. I love you, kiddo.

CONTENTS

ACKNOWLEDGEMENTS

I wanted to start by giving a very special thank you to Neil Thrussell. The idea for this book came about by a great conversation he and I had one afternoon, and the question came up: "how can we make an impact in people's lives that will create long-lasting or everlasting change?". That conversation included an in-depth look at our own lives, including what works, along with what doesn't. From that conversation, we saw a pattern emerging. Four distinct dimensions formed the pillars to our success.

Like myself, Neil is a passionate, driven individual. Desire has always been a strong motivational factor for him, and it's what's catapulted him to where he is in life now. It's because of the Desire, Determination, Dedication, and Discipline that we possess, that we were sparked with the burning passion to share these "secret keys" to success with you.

To find out more about Neil, or to get in touch with him please visit his website at https://shindao.com or e-mail him at info@shindao.com.

I want to thank Tim Summers for providing background information that aided in creating this book, and for supplying his own unique insights.

I want to thank Rachael Verdel for her tireless efforts as my executive coach and keeping me on point for this project. It's because of her unique approach, and her extreme energy and passion that I was able to attack this easily and effortlessly. Thank you, Rach, you are truly a thought leader!

I want to thank Melanie Gessner for allowing me to work with her, utilizing these same principles to manifest her own picture of success. Melanie, you made an incredible guinea pig, and I thank you so very much. I could not have done this without you!

A special thank you to my very best friend, my brother, Doug Rue, for always believing in me. You have always been there for me, through some of the best times and the worst times, yet no matter what, you always had my back. You always saw what I was capable of and it's your support for me, and encouragement of my passion for growing, that continues to drive me forward with unmatched velocity.

I'm incredibly grateful for the people who have made such an impact in my life, including Tony Robbins, Joseph McClendon III, Russell Brunson, Bjorn Ahlen and Anita Koslowski. You have all been instrumental in my transformation to becoming the person I now am today. It's because of the incredible messages that each of you has shared, that I have evolved from living a life of being uncertain and without direction, to a life filled with purpose and passion.

I want to thank my mother-in-law Jewal, for introducing me to the world of Tony Robbins, and for always being there to be my cheerleader. You too saw what I could not see within myself, and you never once gave up on the belief of the impact that I would go on to have on others.

I want to thank my mother Evelyn for being there when I needed her the most. In my darkest hour, you did everything you could to help me carry that burden, and in those times when I felt lost, you were always there to help guide me. I love you, mom.

Lastly, I want to thank my wife, Steffany. Baby, we've been through so much. We've seen the highs, and we've seen the lows, and it's because of each of those experiences that we continue to grow and evolve every day. From the first moment we met, you somehow knew that I would go on to be so much more than who or what I was at that moment, and you were right. Thank you for believing in me and never giving up hope.

INTRODUCTION
WHY WE DO THE THINGS WE DO

CHAPTER 1 - INTRODUCTION

Have you ever been really excited about a particular goal or a particular outcome, yet struggled to find that one secret ingredient to bring it to life? Isn't it true that you may have always wanted to embrace what that goal or outcome fully represented to you, and then *make* it a part of who you are, yet almost every time you set your intent, it seemed that you consistently come up short?

How about time? Does it feel like no matter how hard you work, or how long you work, there's never enough hours in the day to get everything done that you've wanted to? If only there were just a FEW more hours in the day.

Money's another big one. Doesn't it seem like no matter how hard you work, or how long you work, there's never quite enough? That you can make all the right moves, and what appears to be all the right investments, and you still end up short of what your goal was?

Maybe it's that relationship you've craved for so long, the one where you have that perfect partner who shares those same goals and desires as you do. The partner who totally completes you. The one you're still searching for.

Let me tell you a secret – you're not alone!

My name is Jamie Adamchuk, and I used to be in that exact spot. Not just once or twice, but frequently! I was stuck. It wasn't until I figured out and then *put into practice*, the principles of the dimensions of success, that I finally began to live life in a way that was completely fulfilling.

Because success does leave clues, let me take a moment and share a little of my own personal journey with you, so that you may find the proof that you've been searching for; proof that will demonstrate to you beyond a shadow of a doubt that not only is it possible to have what you've always dreamed of and desired, you can actually ENJOY the quest to its attainment. Yes, that's right, actually ENJOY each and every step of the process, including this very first step right NOW!

What is my purpose?

That's the question I used to ask myself over and over. I knew with certainty that I had some greater purpose, however, for the life of me, I couldn't put my finger on what that purpose was, and because of that, I made some pretty crazy choices.

Now at the time, I couldn't tell you with exact clarity as to *why* I asked that very question over and over, I just *knew* that it held some great importance for me. That until I could answer the question of what my true purpose is, I would be left to navigate a world of turbulence. A tumultuous world in which I was the captain of the boat, out in the middle of an ocean, *without a chart or working navigation equipment!* And turbulent the times were!

I had such a desire to have so many new experiences, experiences that I had hoped would lead me to the answer to my burning question, yet no matter how many new things I tried, the answer remained elusive.

What I did learn during this period, is that every time I had a new experience, something that I had never done or seen before, I got a bit of a high. And like every high we have in our lives, I LOVED how it made me feel. How many of you can relate to this?

Unfortunately for me at that time, all my highs would eventually fade, and there I would be again, searching for the next one. I searched so much in fact that it became somewhat of an obsession. I NEEDED to find that next high. It was an absolute must to have those new experiences and all those who stood in my way, or attempted to prevent me from having them, be damned!

Now, I've never been a drug user, however, if this is even just a fraction of what someone who lives that type of lifestyle feels, then let me tell you, I can understand why you'd do just about anything to get that next fix - because it has become a MUST!

What I didn't realize at the time, is that my need to experience more; more love, more passion, more excitement, more joy, was completely destructive because I was seeking to meet it for all the wrong reasons. Every time I found that next high, no matter what the cost, it would drive me to always search for that next step - the step that would indeed take me to that next high, however, would ALSO take me one step further away from everything that I had in my life at that time. That pursuit, chasing that mythical dragon, would ultimately cost me everything that I had worked so incredibly hard to amass, along with my relationship.

Now you might think this is where I finally discovered my purpose and true direction in life. That it took this hard lesson of losing it all to finally smarten up. Because after all, people who've had it all and then lose it all *must* learn from these mistakes, right? Well, if you thought that, unfortunately, you'd be wrong.

Hell NO I didn't learn!! This was now my TIME! I was FREE! I could now pursue my wildest desires without repercussion. Hell YES! This was MY time to GROW - except it wasn't, and I didn't.

Did I have some incredibly wild times? Absolutely! Did I have some experiences that I certainly couldn't write about here because I know beyond a shadow of a doubt that they might embarrass you just by reading about them? Probably. Yet these did nothing to satiate that never-ending need to have, feel, see and experience MORE!

I was trapped in a never-ending circle.

Through all these, I was also caught in a tumultuous divorce and custody battle that dragged on and on, all because it never seemed to go the way I wanted it to. I entered into several relationships which were very short-lived until I stumbled onto the beautiful lady that is now my wife today.

But, what about the question you ask? What about your purpose in life? Was she the one that finally "tamed" you and helped you discover the answer to your question? Is the right woman the solution to all the woes in the world?

Yes... and no.

When I met her, I was still that "guy." Even though I'd love to say that I had changed and improved, and finally learned from all my past failures, I still hadn't. I was still that same old guy on the inside, wearing a different coat on the outside. Isn't it interesting, that by working on only one aspect of who you are, you can develop the appearance of change, and successfully portray that new person, yet to achieve complete, lasting change, you have to be open to work on ALL facets of who you are? Many people become masters of this false change, or surface only changes, being one person on the outside and someone different on the inside, yet they miss out on the true gold of complete transformation.

The first major change came when I finally decided to put Steffany's needs before my own. If you're curious about what that means, go ahead and re-read the last few paragraphs I wrote. Did you notice that everything was very "I" focused? Imagine if "I" had put more value on what others needed, versus my own selfish needs. Do you think that the outcome could have, or would have been very different if I had made that one very small shift?

I think I knew deep down that if I continued doing things the way I always had, things would ultimately end at the same conclusion that they always have, and I knew with certainty that things MUST be different this time. I knew that to continue riding this same roller coaster that I had ridden for so many years, now meant *the certain death* of my relationship, and that was an entirely unacceptable outcome. This was the exact leverage that I needed for myself, to begin to create the change that absolutely had to be made.

When I stopped to listen, to *really* listen to her, things began to transform. No longer was it all about me; it was finally about the both of us.

All I had to do was make that one simple distinction. I had to recognize that it was no longer just me on this ship of relations. I now had a co-captain, and to get to where we were going, without capsizing the boat, I had to be open to someone else' ideas and input, because many times, she was the one with the map! The beauty of sharing this is that right now; anyone can make a choice to change their present condition. All it takes is to look at your circumstance from a different perspective. Look at it from the perspective of a bystander. What would they say about you, and how would they describe your relationship to someone else?

I was just about there; it took only one more push for me to discover the answer that I had sought for so long.

Several years back my wife and I were offered the opportunity to attend a weeklong intensive program designed to break through to your authentic self and enhance your relationship. The speaker is a very prominent figure in the self-empowerment and motivation industry. Well, I did what any other normal red-blooded man would do. I said HELL NO! Why do I need someone to tell me how to run my relationship and my life? My wife kindly let her mom know that I wasn't quite ready to take that next step yet.

Not to be dissuaded, my mother in law sent us a cd program by that same speaker. It took me six months to finally listen to that program, and when I finally did, everything changed. That program set me on a whole new course, to finally answer that burning question, and when that question was answered, everything fell into place and my question, along with my entire life, changed.

Now you might be thinking, what good is that? How is that supposed to help when you have one question answered, yet left with a completely brand new question? Here's the thing. The question I previously had left me directionless, because it was open ended. It lacked the correct definition to engage me in a passionate purpose, and without that passionate purpose, I was constantly stuck seeking something that I couldn't define. For me, it was a true gift to have that initial question answered, and an even greater gift to define my new powerful question, a question that now outlines my life's purpose.

It was through that one cd program, (and then all the rest of the cd programs that were available) and two subsequent live events that we were fortunate enough to attend, that provided the fuel for what I'm about to share with you today. It's the answer to the lack of time in life; it's the answer to the shortage of money that you may be continuously experiencing and it's certainly the answer to living the life that you know you are capable and deserving of living.

Once you see or experience something, you cannot un-see or un-experience it, and fortunately for me, the experiences that I had were all the leverage that I needed for myself to create meaningful, lasting change. These experiences led me to a state of No More. No More would I be left searching for something that I believed was outside my own grasp, because once I realized that belief was completely dis-empowering, I made the decision to change it. I had finally realized that by applying these same tools that I'm about to share with you, I could redesign and transform my life into the life I have always desired. I could easily create the time to spend with those most important to me. I could set and achieve all the goals I have ever wanted. Most importantly, I could have the most incredible relationship with the woman that meant the most to me, not next week, or next month, but *right now!*

No More would I be working a job, that although was easy and provided the means to support my family effortlessly, it provided me absolutely no stimulation or growth. It stifled my creativeness and was not congruent with my new question that I had discovered for my life

No More would I sacrifice my true happiness in life. I had finally recognized that I could have *all* that I wanted out of life and share that same experience with the person that meant the most to me. Now was the time to reach out and pick that low hanging fruit! The season had come, and the fruit was ripe!

No More would I be selfish and only consider my own needs before the needs of those most important to me, because when I discovered that I *could* meet my own needs, simply by meeting the needs of those around me, my life became truly complete. Let me say that one more time because it's *powerful*: When I discovered that I could meet my own needs, by meeting the needs of others, my life became truly complete.

This discovery put in motion a drive within me to duplicate these results, not just for myself, but for others whose lives I had the ability to touch. How could I make this process consistently repeatable, regardless of the desired outcome each individual was seeking? What was the key to it all, so that no matter the desired outcome, there was a standardized process to attain success at each individual's level?

I pondered on these questions long and hard and then it hit me like a ton of bricks. I finally recognized that the recent transformation and shift in my own life was made up of four distinct parts. Desire, Determination, Dedication, and Discipline. I had a *desire* to create a change that I knew beyond a shadow of a doubt absolutely must be made. The need to facilitate this change, this burning desire, provided the fuel for *determination* to step in and see to it that no matter how many roadblocks were set in my path, no matter how many challenges that I would face, I would achieve the outcome that I had set for myself. My high level of *dedication* ensured that no matter how many "other" things popped up, you know, those important things like checking Facebook and playing Candy Crush, there was nothing that could dissuade me from taking the steps to making this critical change. Lastly, it was the *discipline* of sticking to the structure that I set out for myself that truly enabled me to integrate the change into my life fully. Without that 4th D, having that discipline to ensure that every day and every way I was living up to, and when possible exceeding, my success parameters, my newly defined outcome would most likely not have been achieved.

The outcome can be anything that you wanted it to be if you follow this same blueprint – this same pattern. My own success in creating the massive changes that I experienced had left huge clues for me to track, and once I discovered that these clues were actually the pillars of my own success, I knew immediately that it was my duty to share this with all others.

Oh, and my NEW question: How can I help even more people live a life that is free from unnecessary suffering NOW? Quite the change from "What's my purpose in life?"!

I'd like to share one secret with you right now, so that even if, for some strange reason, you choose to not read past this first chapter, (although I know that if you've read this far, and heck, just because you picked up this book, means that you are in that elite group of people who are committed to doing whatever it takes to squeeze the most out of life, and to stop reading at this point would be akin to cutting off your arm) I want you to have something you can put to work right now. Are you ready for it?

Set yourself up for always turning right! (for everyone over on the other side of the pond, and down under, replace right with left).

This idea came to me the other day when Steffany and I were out for a bike ride. Here we were, in a busy urban area, deciding where we wanted to go and what path we wanted to take to get there. After choosing our destination and getting a clear idea of how we get there, along with how we get back, (I'm one of those people who despise going the same way I came, and always look for the best way to make a loop, because I'd much rather see something new, over the same old thing I've already seen) I noticed something. The path we had chosen to take was one of mostly right turns and very few lefts. Of the lefts that we did have to take, they were mostly at the beginning of our route. Sure, there were a few lefts to take, yet it was unmistakable that the route we had chosen was dominated with right turns. It was obvious to me, looking at the route, why we had chosen this path. It was the safest easiest path, that got us to our destination with the least chance of getting in an accident. Sure, there were many different paths we could have chosen, but this path, the one that ensured the least amount of turns in front of vehicles, was the one we chose.

What's most interesting of this, is that we didn't have a conversation about taking the safest path, or consciously chose to take the path that had us turning in front of vehicles the least, we took it because it made sense. We took it because we had learned from past experiences (and a few close calls) that when you set yourself up to always take a majority of right turns, you're immediately putting your best foot forward and setting yourself up for success right from the start, regardless of where your destination is.

When you apply this exact same principle to your own life, you'll be amazed at how much easier life happens for you. Why make a choice to be constantly taking left turns, or paths that provide unnecessary challenges, when instead, you can right now make a choice to discover a new direction by making one simple change. That's truly all it takes. Get clear on your destination, or outcome, and then discover the path to get you there, that takes advantage of the natural flow of traffic.

Now it's true that life isn't always going to flow perfectly, and yes, you'll still have to take a few lefts. Heck, you might even miss your turn, and that's OK! Think of it like this: if you miss that turn, you're being given another opportunity to get to where you need to go, all the while, discovering what great lessons you can now share with others. Seek to find the opportunities in every moment, regardless if it's a missed turn or not, and see, hear, feel and know that your life is growing like never before.

Looking back on my own example and thinking about the multitude of failed relationships I experienced, it's easy to now discover that I was clearly taking left turns and U-turns all the time! I was completely missing out on the prospect of seeing everything for the opportunity that it was. I was constantly looking for shortcuts, and because of that, I was always taking unnecessary risks and missing out on the best part of it all – the journey. I wasn't totally clear on my outcome, or what I truly desired, and because of that, I couldn't see the path I needed to take. It took me having those very experiences, being challenged at every turn, to finally discover what I had to do, what I MUST do. How I now had to change my life. When I finally got clear on exactly who I wanted to attract into my life, what kind of person they would need to be and what character traits they would have to possess, is when I attracted the beautiful lady that is now my wife and soulmate.

Clarity and direction are two of the biggest secrets to a satisfied life. When you get clear on exactly what it is you want, and then take the massive, determined action to specifically lay out your path to success, constantly being aware of opportunities for right turns, you become unstoppable. And when you reach that incredible feeling of being unstoppable, nothing can stand in your way because you have achieved your very own...

SUCCESS

WHAT DOES IT MEAN FOR YOU?

CHAPTER 2 - SUCCESS

What is success? That seems to be a fitting question to begin this entire process. However, my answer to that question is simple - I don't know. Now, WAIT! How can that be? You sold me a book - a book you said contains the processes that are going to bring me great success and you're now telling me that you don't KNOW what success is?

Yes, that's right.... with a caveat: I don't know what success is for <u>YOU</u>!

Success is very individual. Picture it like this: You're a long-term bass fisherman, and you've finally had your dream come together. You're actually fishing in the Bassmaster Elite Series! You feel a pull on your line and, after fighting a great fight, you ultimately land an eighteen-pound largemouth bass. You know for sure that you have this in the bag! You've waited your whole life to land a monster like this, and now here you finally are, and to top it off you're going to win the competition!

Now for some of you, that right there is the picture of success, however, for others, that may not even be something you're interested in. I know for myself, winning the Bassmaster tournament doesn't even make my list of goals or accomplishments, and I also know that many of the goals and accomplishments that I have set for myself may be of no interest to you what so ever.

It's because of this contrast that there's absolutely no way I could ever tell you what success means to you.

Success is very personal. We define our *own* meaning of success as to what it means for each and every one of us. For me to tell you that I'm going to give you success, would make me a bold-faced liar, because success is individual, and I certainly can't tell you what success means to you – only you can do that. What I can tell you, is that four things are consistent with any success, no matter what that success may be, and those are four very specific dimensions – Desire, Determination, Dedication, and Discipline.

Before we jump into that though, let's discuss success a little bit more. How do you know when you've achieved success? What is the key indicator for you to say "Ok...this is a success"?

To know when you have achieved success means that at some time, you must have set a line in the sand and said "when I stand on this side of the line I am yet to be successful. However, when I step over this line, and by stepping over that imaginary line, I at that point accomplish some task or feat, only then can I rate myself as successful." My hallucination is, if that's the way you rank success, then you may find it very elusive and hard to capture.

What if for a moment, you broke down the anatomy of success?

What if instead of seeing each success as the penultimate outcome of some great goal (and isn't it true that ALL of our goals are great – why else would we set them?) What if, for a moment, we saw success as each and every step we took to bring us closer to that great big goal? Would you have a very different experience recognizing and celebrating each and every little win? Would it make your quest that much more exciting? In my humble opinion, I would give that a resounding YES!

But why celebrate the little stuff? Isn't it true that I must save my celebration for the end – to save my merriment for when I have fully achieved what it is that I've set out to accomplish? Unfortunately, whoever came up with that idea is most likely the same person who told you that you couldn't touch or shake or feel your presents before Christmas! That you have to leave them there - having them tempt you with their shiny bows and sometimes large sizes – filled with mystery, yet there is NO TOUCHING! How did your imagination get going when you secretly picked up that box and felt its weight for the first time? Did you have many different thoughts flow through your mind as to what it could be? How about when you shook it a little bit and felt the weight shift in your hands. Did it give you that sense of excitement and wonderment as to what you thought it might be? Did it create a new sense of curiosity within you? I know for myself, sneaking a feeling of my presents always created such a sense of marvel and delight and I would long for the day that I would finally be able to open them.

I say go ahead… break the rules. Give that present a little shake. Celebrate every time you reach a milestone, no matter how big or small, because each time you do, you create greater and greater momentum, and it's that momentum that ensures you accomplish exactly what it is you set out to do in the first place.

How do I know when to celebrate?

Let me share with you the initial creation process for our upcoming program, The 4D's of Success. Neil and I had an idea to do something that truly makes a difference in people's lives. We wanted to create something unique, something dramatic and something life changing. Now because we've both had so many experiences to draw on, both positive and negative, it only made natural sense to use our own lives as examples of how others can use strategic shortcuts to empower their very own lives. It started off with that idea (Celebrate). That Idea then turned into a Facebook page (Celebrate). That Facebook page needed a logo, so one was created (Celebrate). Next, a web page was created (yep… you got it Celebrate). Finally, this book came to life (BIG Celebration). Are you clearly seeing the pattern here? Yes, there is always more work to be done, and with that ongoing work, will be many more celebrations. We both very much look forward to them because without a doubt, it's the celebrations that keep us fully engaged and HUNGRY for the next phase of this incredible journey.

Ok… so I can celebrate my goals, even the little wins, but my goals keep changing! How am I supposed to celebrate the goal when I never seem to hit the net because the net keeps moving?

The very first step in goal setting (Which we cover in our in-depth goal setting workshop) is to get crystal clear on exactly what it is you set out to do. What is the exact outcome that you desire? Get VERY detailed about the entire big picture. What specifically it is you will accomplish? When will you accomplish it? Who will be involved with you accomplishing your goal and lastly, how will your life now be, having accomplished that goal? If you want to get really detailed and take it one step further, imagine how your life will be both one year and three years after accomplishing your goal.

Once you've made it real, almost as though you've already done what you set out to do (I utilize a particular process to associate you with that experience fully) I then discover what your compelling reason is for seeing the goal through to completion. This is better known as "getting leverage on yourself." It's also identifying your compelling reason - the reason that no matter what comes in your way, no matter who puts up roadblocks, you have all the motivation within you to break through anything that may have held you back in the past.

So, what does success mean to you? Can you define it on your terms? Before you read ahead, take a moment and envision what success is for you. Do you see success as completing some great task that has continued to defy completion? Do you see it as finally owning that car you've always desired? Or how about the beachfront cabin or home that you've had your eye on for the last three years?

Is it perhaps finally building that orphanage in Mexico – you know that one that you've always wanted to build, but have lacked these special tools to get you started on your path?

Or is it taking charge of your health and understanding why you feel the way you do?

Maybe it's even attracting that incredible partner into your life – the one that makes your heart sing. The one that you know, beyond a shadow of a doubt, is your true life's soulmate.

The above goals and successes are actual real goals that some of my clients have shared with me, and they have allowed me to use them as examples for YOU to decide on exactly what success *could* look like for you.

If you were successful in defining your success, and what that ultimate success looks like for you, congratulations! This would be an incredible time for a celebration!

For those of you who weren't able to see what your success looks like for you, or you can see something that may look like success, however, it's not as clear as you'd like, I'd like to take a moment and share with you some of the reasons why.

For the longest time, money eluded me. There was never enough, and when I did have it, it never seemed to last. It felt as though I was only ever able to make it to a certain level, and once I had achieved that level, that was it! There was no pushing past that magically invisible ceiling no matter how much harder I worked or how many extra hours I put in. This completely baffled me. How was it possible that even when I was able to make just a little extra, something always seemed to come up that made sure I stayed at that level? Extra course fees, a new water heater, a leak in the roof. All things popped up right around that same time that I had just a little extra cash set aside. And then it dawned on me: What if I'm only making what I need to make?

When I reflected on my current and past situation, I recognized that I was never behind on any bills and always had almost exactly what I needed, never a lot more, and not less.

When I was growing up there was never an abundance of money. I lived in a single income home where there was always food on the table, and we always had a roof over our heads. We even had some of the luxuries in life, like a VCR; however, we would never be described as well off. We weren't the family who went to Disneyland, or really any other trip for that matter. We were the family who had just what we needed, never more and never less. My mom worked hard to make sure that we were always taken care of, and I always went to school well dressed, sometimes I suspect, when she couldn't really afford it. This was my life growing up.

Isn't it interesting how that same pattern of psychology surrounding money followed me into my very own life?

At the time, that pattern surrounding money was the only one that I knew of, and because of that, it's the pattern I chose to live with. Yes, that's right, chose to live with. I know it's a choice because when I finally recognized that if I wanted to get ahead, I had to develop an entirely new belief system when it came to money. I had to believe that it was OK to have money. I had to challenge and completely destroy the limiting beliefs around what I felt it would mean to have money. I had to recognize, that to have money would not make me a bad person, rather, enable me to live and share my soul purpose with so many more people.

I had to stop being *afraid* of money.

Because we didn't have a lot of excess money (ok, no excess money) when we were growing up, and thinking about how my parents spoke about some of the people who did have money, I linked it up in my mind that to have money must mean that you are a person of questionable integrity, and to have just what you need, is the "right" way to live. This wasn't something that I consciously thought of, or planned to do, it just happened.

When I finally uncovered that subconscious limiting belief surrounding money and then destroyed that belief, I was able to replace it with a new empowering story that ultimately changed my entire life. I allowed myself to recognize that having money didn't make me any less of a person. I wasn't a "bad" person for having money, because with having this new resource, this extra cash, I could now make a difference in so many more people's lives.

Several things happened when I changed my beliefs. The first was the creation of my new story surrounding having money. The new story that told me I wasn't someone who had questionable integrity for having money. The new story that said having money doesn't mean pain, because when you have a story that dictates something negative about a certain circumstance you will do everything you can, either consciously aware or not, to avoid that pain. My new story set me up for truly being open to success in that part of my life.

The second thing I did, was to change my reference to what I could do, once I had attracted the money into my life. What that means is that I now gain massive pleasure from being able to contribute to others on a level that I had never been able to before. Having that money meant that I could help even more people live their life free from unnecessary suffering, and for me, that's is what life is all about. For me, seeing that specific outcome, and recognizing that by having this additional money I could easily and effortlessly achieve my true purpose and passion, was all the drive that I needed to change my pattern. I had achieved my success. I saw the specific outcome that I must have, and why I must have it. I recognized what was holding me back and I discovered my very own compelling reason for making success the only option. I was so clear on exactly what my outcome would be, that it was impossible for anything to stand in my way.

The last thing I did was reflect on what it would mean not to have that money. I asked myself how my life would be different if I didn't have the resources I need to help others. I saw a very dismal future. One where I continued to work that nine to five job, never meeting my full potential, never being able to help the people that I knew I was put here for. I saw myself stuck in that grind, totally defeated. I physically felt what it would be like to live that life for the remainder of my days. That right there was, even more, leverage for me to create that change. Seeing that life, devoid of satisfaction, was the very last straw that I needed to manifest my new future.

In the end, it wasn't about having the extra money or having a whole bunch of new toys; it was about what I could do now that I had it. For me, doing what I do is my very own model of success, and because of that, I am relentless in its pursuit.

Success is always set on your terms and in your language. It's the path you take to obtain your success that can make or break your desired outcome. The first step on the path to your success is the first of the four dimensions, and that is...

DESIRE
THE 1st DIMENSION

CHAPTER 3 - DESIRE

Desire: **1. To wish or long for, crave, want.**
2. A longing or craving, as for something that brings satisfaction or enjoyment.

Have you ever desired something in your life... really desired something? Maybe it was asking that beautiful lady, who is now your wife, out on that first date, or finding the perfect house to call yours. Or maybe it was discovering that the new Tesla Model S is now the fastest production car in the world and you just HAVE to get yourself one?

Whatever your desire is, let me ask you this: what would you be willing to do, to guarantee that your desire would become your reality?

Let that thought circulate in your mind for a moment or two.

Dreams create desires. Whenever you've had a desire in your life, it was created from a dream of having exactly what it is that you desired. Think about that. When you first had the desire to ask that beautiful lady out on a date, did you see yourself walking arm and arm or hand in hand together? Did you wonder what it would feel like when you shared that first kiss, smelling that faint hint of perfume on her perfect skin? I strongly believe that at that moment, in that magical moment of dreaming what it would be like to have those experiences for yourself, you created a desire. A desire that burned so strongly within you that you had to make it a reality.

Maybe your desire is something else. Maybe you desire to become the CEO of your own company, or to live on a yacht, or to own that million-dollar house. Whatever that desire it, it started with a dream.

One of the most impactful dreams created a desire, and that desire created a change that had never before been experienced in all of history. Those famous words "I have a dream" created such a massive desire in people to create a shift of epic proportions. That shift lives on today, all because one man uttered those powerful words. Words that would forever change the shape and social structure of humankind.

Now I don't know about you, but if one man can get so certain and change millions of people's lives, doesn't it not only seem possible, or probable that you have the ability within you to change your life? I mean, after all, it's just one life we're talking about here. Not millions like the change Dr. Martin Luther King's speech created, but just one – yours.

Ask yourself the question. Are you worth it? Now whoa… am I worth it? Who are you talking to here? What do you mean "am I worth it"? I mean exactly that – are you worth it? Are you worth discovering what your dream is? Are you worth the effort to take that dream and manifest it into what you have always desired? Are you worth the effort it will take to shift your life now, into the life you've always craved? This question is the defining question in your quest, because if you're not worth it, or *worthy* of the dream and desire, then change your focus now. Change it because a dream that you feel you're not deserving of is a dream and desire that you will never attain.

Heck of a question, isn't it? It's supposed to be. It's designed to get you to really think about that desire and understand if it's something you're willing to go for – something that you're *ready* to go for. If you're not ready to burn that midnight oil then you're not ready to hit that goal, but if you are, then buckle in, because it's going to be one hell of a ride.

Next question – is the outcome worth it? Now you might say "Well, of course, it's worth it! It's my dream!!" Is it really though? I ask that because I think of a story of two farmers who both had the same goal of owning one thousand sheep.

In this story, there were two farmers who both had a dream and desire of owning one thousand sheep. Farmer number one had struggled for a long time to build his farm, faced numerous hardships along the way, yet persevered in growing his farm and the size of his herd. Slowly but steadily the count of his sheep increased, yet the profitability of the farm remained in question. None the less his goal was always to reach one thousand sheep. Farmer number one always kept an eye on farmer number two's herd and saw how quickly it was increasing, and became almost obsessed with keeping up and doing whatever he could to always be matching what farmer number two was doing.

Farmer number two, who also had this same dream, and faced the same initial struggles, watched his herd grow much more quickly and saw a marked increase in his profitability. He re-invested back into his farm wisely and continue to grow his herd count. Before farmer number two knew it, he had reached his goal of having one thousand sheep.

Here you have two farmers who have the same goal, who started out with the exact same means, who have the same desired outcome, yet are experiencing different results.

Why do you think that is?

The answer is simple: Because of their desired outcome. Here's the rest of the story.

Some time back, farmer number one was visiting the local watering hole and had overheard that farmer number two had a goal to own one thousand sheep. Farmer number one, not to be outdone, had in that moment cast that same goal for himself. He knew that he was the first sheep farmer in town and to have farmer number two come in and outdo him would be unacceptable.

What farmer number one didn't hear was the *reason* farmer number two had this great lofty goal.

Farmer number two did indeed have the goal of having one thousand sheep. Not to be the biggest sheep farmer in town, but to be able to meet the demand of wool for clothing that was being manufactured for an orphanage in the next town over. You see, in the area where farmer number one and farmer number two lived, it got quite cold in the winter. Farmer number two had grown up in an orphanage in a similar part of the country and experienced many a cold winter. It was his vow never to experience another winter freezing as he had, that stoked his fire to make sure that no child would ever have to face those same hardships.

In working with the orphanage, farmer number two had also discovered a market for mutton that was previously untapped, and because of that, he was able to both meet his need for contribution, and at the same time profit from his deep-seated goal to help others. The goal was never about having to make the most money, or about having the most sheep. His goal was about meeting a need that profoundly benefited others. It just so happened that to meet that need efficiently, the magic number was one thousand sheep.

Although their goals of having one thousand sheep were the same, the purpose behind the goal was very different, and it's that purpose, that outcome, that drove farmer number two to be as successful as he was. Not for selfish profit, but to make a difference in the lives of others. To stand out among the rest for what he was doing and to help others.

You see, the ultimate success factor is the impact you can have on others. When your outcome serves not only yourself, but it ALSO serves to meet the needs of others around you, instantly that desire burns brighter. Instantly that desire moves to the top of the list because it's no longer just you depending on the outcome, it's others who are also depending on that same outcome.

Now we're not saying that every single outcome you desire must have other people's needs attached to it. But if you want to get massive leverage on yourself, that level of leverage that commits you two hundred percent, if you want to have all the desire possible, then go ahead – be brave and set a goal that serves a greater purpose other than just your own.

So, we ask you again – is your goal, or outcome, worth it? Does it have the ability to have a significant, profound effect on those around you? Can your ultimate outcome make a difference in something greater than you?

Give this a whirl. Next time you have a desire that you must have, ask yourself the question: What class of experience is this? Would the outcome be a class four experience, that being it doesn't feel good, it is not good for you, it is not good for others, and it doesn't serve the greater good? Now I know you might be thinking "why the heck would I want to have a class four experience?" Believe me, that's a great question, yet people seem to have them every single day! Think of a class four experience as a bad or abusive relationship. You wake up every day to someone you no longer love. The moment you get up you're being criticized for not spending enough time together. You attempt to smooth the waters yet the more you do, the more you get yelled at, and before you know it, you hear a thumping on the wall because the argument has woken up the neighbors next door. Your partner continues to berate you until you head off to work where you reflect on the morning's events. Because you're so focused on those events, you fail to make the sales that you needed to enable the company to hit the month end targets that it had established. Can you imagine a person's level of desire in this type of relationship? How successful do you think a person in this situation would be at creating and maintaining a peak state? Well, unless that desire is to change the situation and find a new relationship, success would all but be impossible.

Is your outcome a class three experience where it feels good, but is NOT good for you, is not good for others and does not serve the greater good? This class of experiences could best be related to a heroin addict. Now as I said earlier, I've never been a drug user, but if I were to imagine what it must be like I'd picture it something like this. There's excitement behind getting that high because it feels so good and it takes all the pain away. That peaceful state where no one can touch you and no one matters because at that moment it's all about you. Yes... at that moment it sure feels good, yet, what about after that high wears off? How about that feeling you get when you find yourself searching for what you can sell to get that next hit, how, when it's been too long between fixes you curl up into a ball and vomit all over yourself because your body is detoxing. How in those moments you can't help anyone because you can barely help yourself? Yes... it feels great when you first get it, yet afterward, when that high has worn off, you feel like death warmed over. Ok yes... that's a pretty extreme example, yet if you associate a class three experience to something so disgusting that you would NEVER do it, then chances are if you discover that the ultimate outcome would result in class three, there's no WAY you'd even consider going down that path.

Perhaps the outcome is a class two experience: It doesn't feel good, but it IS good for you, it IS good for others, and it DOES serve the greater good? Class two experiences are GREAT experiences to have because they give you the magic of growth! This is truly one of the occurrences in life where all the rewards live. Yes, that's absolutely right. Think of this as a real-life experience. You're married to a beautiful shapely partner. You're the CEO of a Fortune Five Hundred Company. You commit some of your free time to your local church. You have a beautiful family who loves you deeply, and you have all the toys you've ever wanted. Everything in your life is *almost* picture perfect, except for that spare tire around your middle that seems to grow a little larger every year. Your partner notices this about you, and because they're so incredibly in love with you, they want to help you out. Because you've done so well in your life, you, of course, happen to have a small personal gym in your house. Your partner tells you that they are concerned for your health, and they want to do everything they can for you to ensure that you lead a long and healthy life. What this means, is that from this day forward you'll need to get up one hour earlier and work out with your partner. P.S. Remember how shapely your partner is? How could you possibly say no to that?

You agree to begin this new regime and even agree to change some of your eating habits. Now if you're like me that first day back on the equipment was a killer, and taking my greens... yuck! I knew that this new exercise regime sure didn't feel good at all, yet I also knew that it was good for me, because it was going to get me back into shape, even though people kept telling me that round was a shape! I knew that it was good for others because if I had stayed on the same path, there's no doubt that I would not be around for as long as others wanted me to be. I also knew that it served the greater good because when I was able to get my body into a healthier peak state, I was able to serve at a level that I hadn't been able to serve at for a long time.

A funny thing happened after a couple of months of suffering through this crazy new morning ritual… I actually began to enjoy it and look forward to it. That was the day that I finally recognized that this class two experience had now turned into a class one experience

This class one experience now feels good, it is good for me, it is good for others, and it enables me to serve the greater good.

A class one experience is the penultimate goal of achieving a lasting compelling desire, and that's the secret! Set a goal and create a desire that you must absolutely have. An outcome that you desire so much that you will do almost anything to see it through to its fulfillment. That's where the juice in life lies. That's where the true spice of life lives. It's those goals and desires that create such an excitement within you that virtually ensures there is no other possible outcome, other than their attainment!

Coming back to our earlier question, let me ask you again. What would you now be willing to do, to guarantee that your desire will become your reality? What could you do, to get into that peak state, that very special place, where dreams are fueled by the unwavering certainty that they will manifest no matter what? What class two experience can you take right now, and work to turn into a class one experience? Can you clearly see the outcome of your desire and what it will mean to you and the others who will share in its successful outcome?

Here's one other thing to consider. Even before the exercising became a class one experience, I had already stepped into the next phase of the 4D's, because I had...

DETERMINATION
THE 2ND DIMENSION

CHAPTER 4 - DETERMINATION

Determination: **A positive emotional feeling that involves persevering towards a difficult goal.**

How many of you remember the story of The Little Engine Who Could? If you don't remember this story, it's about a trainload of toys and delicious food destined for a village over on the other side of the mountain. The engine that was hauling this bountiful load of joy suddenly stopped working and couldn't move another inch. All the toys that were in the cars jumped out and begged other engines to tow this important shipment over the mountain; however, all the other engines they asked were far too important or too busy to haul the cars over the mountain.

At last a small blue engine came chuffing into the yard, and when the clowns approached, the engine stopped to listen to their plight. After understanding what was required and expressing that she was only a small engine, she chose to do something she had never done before, and haul the load of cars over the mountain.

When the little blue engine came to the big mountain she continued to tell herself "I think I can, I think I can I think I can," and before she knew it, she was at the top of the mountain. She was able to make sure all the food and toys were delivered to their intended recipients. Yes, this is indeed a children's fable; however, it describes in perfect detail *exactly* what determination is. Determination is completely owning the attitude that no matter what comes up, no matter what obstacle is placed in your path you WILL accomplish your goal because, for you, the accomplishment of that goal is SUCCESS.

Seems like a pretty simple principle, right?

Let me ask this question one more time: Is your goal or outcome worth it?

Let's face it. There are things in our lives that we set out to do and never accomplish. Why do you think that is?

The answer to that is simple, because that goal or that intended outcome didn't present itself to you as a true potential outcome, and because of that, there is no excitement, no juice behind it. And when there is no passion for accomplishing the goal, there is absolutely no determination to accomplish what you set out to do. Sure, maybe at first there was some excitement around the possibility of what you had hoped for the intended outcome, however, somewhere along that path something popped up and redefined your need to attain that specified outcome. Maybe it was something that someone said to you, or maybe it was that a circumstance had arisen in your life that changed the need to have that outcome.

Or maybe, just maybe, the reason for your original desire for that goal wasn't all that important after all.

It's pretty easy to see how and why, without an adequate level of both desire and determination, success can be elusive.

Thinking back to the story of the two sheep farmers, each having the same goal, yet each having very different reasons for achieving success, it's easy to understand how determination plays a major factor in the ultimate outcome for each of them. Think for a moment about the amount of leverage they had on themselves. Farmer number one's primary leverage was significance – being the largest sheep farmer in town, whereas farmer number two's leverage was based on never having another child have to face the same circumstances that he had when growing up. That difference right there gave Farmer number two a massive advantage with respect to the level of determination that was available to him. When success gets linked up to a personal aspect, something so personal that to not achieve it will equal massive pain, the impossible becomes possible.

Take a moment now and think back to a time when you accomplished something that you had set out to do. Maybe it was a massive project at work, or maybe it was getting that term paper completed. Maybe it was even finding the person of your dreams, that person who is now your partner for life. Whatever it was, go back in your mind's eye and see yourself working towards the attainment of that outcome you experienced.

As you see yourself taking the steps you took, can you identify the particular moments when you knew, even before you had achieved your outcome, that you would be successful? That you were so certain in your mind that there could be no other outcome, and that it would be the one true final result? This feeling, this certainty, and knowing, is one of the major factors in fueling determination.

What if you could amplify and magnify that feeling, and be able to draw on its energy at any time? Would that be of value? Would that help to fuel your determination, with not just eighty-seven octane fuel, but with ninety-four octane fuel? Yes, it can, and yes it will!

Here's an exercise that you can practice to help build this mental muscle. And just like building muscle, it takes practice, so practice this often. Think of it as your mental workout.

Once you've specifically defined what it is that you're going to achieve, close your eyes and see yourself at the conclusion of your quest to achievement. Picture it vividly... exactly how you'll feel at that moment, knowing that you have now fully completed what you set out to do. You may even notice how your body begins to feel more relaxed, because the weight of expectation, the weight of responsibility of needing to complete the goal, has now passed. What does it mean for you and what does it mean for others now that you've completed something that was once only a dream?

While you are reflecting on this, can you also see how your life is now different for having completed the task?

By doing this same exercise, every time you set out to accomplish a task, you create a memory within your body – a memory providing you proof that you can achieve what it is you're about to do.

Now I know you're probably thinking "how can I have a memory of something I've never even done? Is this guy on crack?" My answer is most definitely no to the crack, and yes... you can have a memory of something you've never done. Crazy idea, right? Let me explain. Your mind is an incredibly powerful tool. So powerful in fact, that it has the ability to create things out of the seemingly thin air. Here's the kicker. Your mind does not have the ability to differentiate between what's real and what isn't! It's true! Use this to your advantage, because when you vividly imagine something, with all the details of exactly what it will be like when you accomplish it, you immediately begin to create that incredible muscle memory. You physically see, hear, feel and know what it's like to have accomplished that task, and once you've done that, you can manifest your outcome with certainty, *because you've already experienced its completion!!*

Think of all the inventions and new ideas over the last hundred years. If no one dared to exercise their minds, would we have any of the technology, or things that we have today? These things and ideas came into being because someone had a goal to make a change. Those thought leaders took their ideas, and through tireless determination (and many failures) saw to it that they achieved their outcome. They may not have had every step planned out, or may not have even known the first step to take! But they had that passion, desire, and determination and knew that no matter how many revisions it took, they would achieve their outcome because they knew they must.

You CAN create the perfect outcome for yourself because YOU are in charge of exactly what happens. You get to say exactly how everything turns out.

While you are practicing this exercise, think of how many different aspects or modalities you can add when you envision your outcome. What kind of day is it outside? Is it summer or winter? Can you smell the flowers, or do you instead feel the bitter chill of the cold? Do you hear the birds chirping in the sky, or is that thunder in the background? Who's with you as you celebrate the culmination of all your hard work? Get completely fully associated with that moment and build the unstoppable momentum that continually fuels your determination.

One of my favorite stories about determination comes from Col. Harlan Sanders. Maybe you've heard of him. Here is a guy who, in his sixties, had the idea of selling his secret recipe for Kentucky Fried Chicken. The idea came to Col. Sanders after receiving some of his first social security payments for a meager one hundred and five dollars. He had the idea to hop in his station wagon, grab his one suit and tour the country looking for someone to partner with in selling his delicious recipe and unique method for cooking his mouthwatering chicken.

Now if you haven't heard this story, and have ever been to KFC, you'd think that was no big task! After all, the chicken is mighty tasty.

Unfortunately, you'd be wrong.

It took one thousand and nine rejections for Col. Sanders to finally receive his first yes. Think about that for just one moment. One thousand and nine no's. Wow. Now if there's ever been someone who is the poster child for determination, Col. Sanders would be it.

You see, he could have given up at any time. He could have said that at sixty-five it was time for him to slow down and enjoy his retirement, yet he did nothing of the sort. Col. Harlan Sanders had the dream of being able to share his secret recipe with the world, and due to his perseverance, his dedication to that specific outcome, there was nothing that could stand in his way.

If one old guy, with virtually no resources, with only one white suit and with just a recipe and a pressure cooker in his car can persevere through over one thousand rejections and then go on to become one of the most recognized faces of all time, what are you capable of? What could you develop, or design or create that would benefit both yourself and those around you? Think of how many more resources you now have, because other thought leaders just like yourself had the courage and determination to make a change, thereby providing you with so many more tools than those who came before you ever had.

What could you do if you truly set your mind to it?

This is the exact question I asked myself after uprooting my life, selling my house and buying a newer bigger house in a new city, and then finding out that the job I had completely redesigned my life for, was no longer there.

Wow. Talk about a life defining moment.

For me, that was the defining moment I recognized that I needed to step up for myself.

Don't get me wrong here. I was shocked. How is it possible, that this company, who I had given my blood sweat and tears for, who I had completely committed to (and who I had actually put before my family at times) could do something like this TO me. Sure. They helped me with the move, and I have to give credit where credit is due; however, they knew what was on the line for me making such a significant move.

Can you see how easy it may have been to get stuck in the blame game at this point? To surrender myself to disempowering actions that would in no way benefit me or any greater good?

How easy do you think it would have been at that point for me to throw my hands in the air and say "I give up!"? "I'm going to wallow in my pity because there's nothing I can do." Well, depending on if you've ever been through an experience like this, may sway the answer to either one side of the equation or the other.

I gave myself one hour to process these feelings – and that was being generous. I now have the ability to change that un-resourceful state into a resourceful one within ninety seconds, however, at that time, I needed just a bit longer.

I sent a few emails to some of my closest work colleagues letting them know the news. I cleared out my desk, handed in my security access and then I was on the road… and you know what? I felt free. I felt free for the first time in a long time, and I made the decision at that moment that never again would I be in a situation like this. Never again would I be at the mercy of someone higher up the food chain, because never again did I want to be completely reliant on someone else to meet so many of my needs. No longer would anyone be in charge of my destiny, other than myself.

I was completely determined that from that point onward, life would be lived on my terms. And ever since that day, I have lived life exactly like that. What's really great about that day, is that's also the day that my true passion got fully cemented within me. I knew that I was meant for more and finally, I had been given this incredible opportunity to get out and follow that passion. To finally use the skills that I had always had, for what I always wanted to use them for - to make a difference in people's lives.

I also recognized that at the moment I received the "bad news," I had felt that things were happening TO me when in reality, life was happening FOR me. It took that experience for me to recognize that one door had indeed closed, yet another one was opening right before me. Not only did I have all the determination I now needed, I also had...

DEDICATION
THE 3RD D

CHAPTER 5 - DEDICATION

Dedication: The quality of being dedicated to a task or purpose.

Before we jump in too deep here I want to clarify one point: Sharing my story with you of losing my job is not designed to have you rush into work and quit your job! Yes, for me it was an incredibly liberating moment of growth; having a moment of reckoning so to speak because life was happening FOR me at that exact time.

So, what does that mean life was happening for me? All too often when something happens, we ask the question: "Why did that happen to me?". We instantly get into a state of defense looking to protect ourselves. It's a subconscious process that many of us do without even recognizing it. What also happens, is when you ask that specific question, your brain MUST answer it. It will look for and seek out any answer that it can to satisfy the equation, and most times, you're left in a disempowering state.

Try this out. Again, think of a moment in time when you had an experience where something didn't work out as you had hoped or expected, and then ask yourself, why did this happen to me. My guess is that you can think of at least one hundred different ideas of why it happened to you. Some of the most common answers are:

- I'm not good enough
- I'm not smart enough
- I didn't have all the tools to do my job
- It wasn't my fault
- The situation was unfair

With answers like those, it's very easy to see how anyone could start their very own society of sorrow! By asking this one simple, seemingly innocent question, you have the ability to single-handedly crush anything positive that could have come out of this experience.

Now try this one: Why is this happening FOR me? Do you get the same need to answer this question in a self-depleting or self-deprecating way? Well, I don't know about you, but if I try to insert one of the previous answers to this specific question, it just doesn't make sense!

When the question "Why is this happening FOR me?" is asked, the most common answers are:

- So that I can learn something
- So that I know what to do better next time
- So that I don't make the same mistake next time

Can you see and feel the significant difference in the outcome simply by changing the question? There really is some merit to the old adage, ask a better question and get a better answer.

Now if you're just a little bit crazy like me, and you know with certainty that you have what it takes to jump in head first and make that level of change, don't let me stop you! Take that leap now, because the longer you wait, the more excuses you'll find as to why things are ok the way they are, even though your true hearts feelings know better.

To make this level of change like I did took a lot of guts. Ok... maybe my situation was slightly different because I lost my job; however, the level of dedication it took to not only survive but THRIVE in this new uncharted world was incredible.

There were indeed times in the beginning when money was tight, and I asked myself "wouldn't it be easier to go get another job?". It could have been so easy just to pick up where I left off and be reliant upon someone else to take care of my best interests.

You know what's interesting? I even tried it once – just to prove to myself what I already knew, except for this time I did it under the guise of a contractor. I felt that by going in as a contractor – having the company hire my company, rather than hiring me as an employee, I would still retain the guise of self-independence and would still serve the clients that I did have.

What I actually did was allow just a smidgen of doubt to enter the door, and by letting that one small part of doubt in, I immediately eroded the level of dedication I had towards my goal of serving others. I had regained the certainty of a steady paycheck, yet at the same time, sacrificed what made me feel the absolute best in life. I recognized at that time I was just a whore for money. That might seem a little strong, but how was I really any different than a prostitute? I was sacrificing my true happiness, and my true life's calling all for the mighty dollar.

I lied to myself for a while, telling myself the story that it was the company that was getting paid, that I was doing a good thing, and that I wasn't betraying what I stood for. Yet, every day that I went in, at the same time and sat at the same desk, a little piece of me began to die. I didn't notice it at first, probably because I was too wrapped up in the story I was telling myself, and the more we tell ourselves a story, the more we begin to believe it.

I even began to justify myself that being unable to serve my personal clients was ok because I was serving a bigger client.

Every day I would make the commute to and fro, and every day I would come home just a little grumpier than the day before. I began to feel worse... physically worse. I was frustrated that even though there were specific tasks I was contracted to do, I was relegated to being a document writer – something I absolutely despised at the time.

Things were coming to a head, and I knew a change was required, yet the lure of that steady income kept teasing me... giving me just enough excitement for me to keep towing the line.

And then my life changed yet again.

I met Tony Robbins.

You remember early on when I said I had the opportunity to attend a weeklong seminar by a renowned self-improvement "guru"? Yep...it was Tony Robbins. Even though I had turned down the initial opportunity, after spending hundreds, if not thousands of hours listening to each and every one of his cd's, I knew that now it was a must to see him live.

I began looking for where he would be next, and as it turned out, Dallas Texas was the next stop where he would be hosting his Unleash the Power Within ("UPW") event. After consulting with Steffany's mom as to which tickets we should purchase, she made it very clear that to have the best experience you need the best tickets. You need to be right up at the front because being in that spot will provide you the richest possible experience.

The price of those tickets was a significant investment; however, this is something I trusted my mother-in-law on because she has been to many of Tony's seminars. In fact, she had the opportunity to personally get to know Tony before he was the superstar that he is today. You see, when Tony first started, things weren't quite as big and grand as they are now, and because of that, the seminars were on a much more intimate level. Quite often, after everything was done for the day, they would all go out for dinner together. I've got to say; I'm just a touch jealous about her having had those incredible opportunities; however, I know with certainty that not too long in future I'll have that same opportunity for myself.

I had my first "premonition" as to what the future held for me when I went to inform my superior that I would be unavailable for the period of time that I would be away for UPW. My first clue came when I was hauled into one of the directors' offices with my then "boss," and it was demanded that I justify my request for time away. Now the big difference between an employee and a contractor is that an employee is entitled to a certain amount of time off with pay, whereas a contractor only need provide their availability. Any time not working on the client's tasks is time unpaid. This was a big one for me, as on that day I clearly understood that my position with that company was viewed as one of an employee relationship and not a contractor. POP. That was the sound of my bubble breaking. I knew right there that all the guise I had been working under – saying to myself that the work I was doing was for my business and that I was still serving my purpose, was complete BS. I knew right there that I had sacrificed my dedication to my greater purpose of making a difference in other people's lives.

Even though I had this feeling of betrayal to myself, I knew that dedication still lived within me, and despite how much I felt I needed the certainty of the ongoing steady paycheck, I knew that attending my mentors live seminar was much more important. I politely let the client know that I would indeed be unavailable for the time that I would be in Dallas, and if that situation didn't work, I would understand if they felt they needed to bring someone else on in place of me. I didn't do it maliciously, I did it with integrity, and that made all the difference in the world.

You see, if I had gone in filled with ego and piss and vinegar, I'm certain I would have had a very different outcome. Not only did the client agree to the time away, but they also recognized the many additional hours I had put in without charge, and actually paid me for that time away. That moment was good and bad - good because it was unexpected money and bad because it kept putting that carrot out in front of the cart. See... it wasn't so bad there - they actually cared about me (or so I thought at the time).

Finally, the day came. We were on the airplane headed for Dallas Texas.

Now for those of you who've been to see Tony live you know what I'm about to say. This seminar was a freaking rock show! I'd never been to anything quite like this in my life! There was music.... LOTS of music. There was dancing. There were more hugs and more high fives than I can count. This was by far the biggest party that I had even been to that didn't include an ounce of liquor.

There was also fire... and I walked on it. Yes, that's right I walked on fire. Part of Tony's experience is the Firewalk which teaches you how to overcome fear. Think about that for a moment: Laying in front of you is a glowing pile of coals between 1800°F - 2000°F and you've got to place your feet on it. Not only place your feet on it but do it over and over till you get to the end of the fire!?! Are you freaking crazy?

Not to build too much drama into the story, but it was dark outside. We were all chanting YES, YES, YES, over and over as we made our way to the fire. The drums were beating in the background like some savage ritual was about to be performed. Before I knew it, I was toes to the fire. It was my turn to walk.

And suddenly everything got really calm. I stepped off of the grass and onto the fire and casually walked to the other end. I didn't run, I didn't freak out, and lo and behold, I didn't get burnt. Not even a single blister.

Now this experience was pretty spectacular. It absolutely showed me what was possible and how careful to be about assigning fear to just anything. I learned that just because one person says something (like the guy who we ran into at the hotel saying how crazy we were and that we'd be in the hospital that night, left with burnt, charred stumps for feet), you have to live the experience for yourself. You have to look FEAR (False Evidence Appears Real) in the face and say, "Just because you were able to exert your force over that one person, or group of people doesn't give you the right to do the same with me!".

As incredible of an experience as the Firewalk was, it wasn't the experience that really hit it home for me. It was the Dickens Process that transformed my life.

Without going into too much detail, and ruining the process before you have your own experience, let me just say that it provided the insights I needed to clearly identify what I must do, and also, what I would no longer stand for. It was this process that took my level of dedication from a seven to a twelve, and that's pretty awesome for a scale that only goes to ten!

Since having attended UPW, I've also had the privilege of attending Tony's Date with Destiny, and Business Mastery. These are truly life changing programs, and many of the breakthrough's and insights I've had at these seminars have empowered me to take these very steps, and share them with you in such a profound way.

Once I returned home, it wasn't long before I found myself giving my notice. Yes, part of that decision was because I was truly unhappy with what I was doing; however, the most important part is that I was now dedicated completely one hundred and ten percent to following my true passion in life - helping others remove the unnecessary suffering from theirs.

It took that one incredible experience for me to put it all together. It took me getting intimately close with my biggest fears and my most dis-empowering beliefs. It took me standing up for what I already knew and believed inside, to finally make the changes that I knew were absolutely critical to make. For me, this moment solidified that dedication to never again go back to a place where I was doing things just to satisfy a short-term need. I knew that to do anything like this, would be like death to my soul. I had finally recognized that to live my true life of happiness, where both myself and those around me would live a life of true satisfaction, I had to follow the only path that was right for me. I had to follow my true passion and calling and never again be tempted by something that I wasn't truly soulfully dedicated to.

That's the absolute truth for me, and when you find that groove, that magical place where everything fits together so perfectly, and everything flows exactly as it was meant to, you'll know that you've also arrived at that special place. For me, being able to make a difference in the people's lives who needed it the most has and continues to overfill my bucket of contribution. In chapter eight of this book, I'm going to share with you a powerful self-assessment tool known as the six human needs. But for now, let me say that when I identified just how many of my needs I could meet, simply by changing the way I interacted with those around me, my life flipped itself on its head and I've *never* looked back.

You see, there was never a need *to* look back. I had absolutely no reason to seek what was already left in the past because of my new path. The new journey that I was on, continually fed me exactly what I was looking for *each and every day!* I had no desire to step backward and live a life that served me no purpose other than to bring me pain. I was (and still am) completely dedicated to the new path that I have discovered because it is my own personal class one experience!

What's the one thing that you would, or could dedicate yourself to today? Does that dedication serve to meet your greater purpose in life? If you were to change how you thought about your desired outcome and got completely certain on what it will mean to you as you now achieve it, does it compound the level of dedication you're willing to put towards its attainment? How does your ultimate destiny now change when the only outcome you see, is the one where you're one hundred and ten percent dedicated to both achieving and living the life you specifically designed for yourself?

This dedication to share what I've learned is actually the main reason Neil and I teamed up to create the program: The 4D'S of Success. It's that same level of dedication that we share, that leads us to ask the question: If we can have this much impact individually, how much impact can we have together? Pretty great question if I do say so myself. Once we had decided that together we can make a much bigger impact, it was only a matter of discipline to bring it all together.

DISCIPLINE
THE 4TH D

CHAPTER 6 - DISCIPLINE

Discipline: **When one uses reason to determine the best course of action, regardless of one's desires, which may be the opposite of excited.**

The 4th D and perhaps one of the most important is discipline. Discipline is all about the structure behind achieving your success. Discipline is about setting a time every day to ensure that you are in that absolute peak place, that both your body and mind are ready willing and able to take the exact steps to see to it that nothing can stand in your way, that nothing can prevent you from achieving your success.

So, what could this look like? Well, for myself, I set out time every morning to reflect and reimagine my goals. I have a very specific process where I fully associate myself with that achievement state, that state where I've already accomplished what I set out to do and then magnify that moment. I look for things I had never noticed before.

Maybe it's a new person that's there that I hadn't noticed before, or maybe it's something about where I am. Every day I re-live that success state, firstly to create that memory muscle, thereby reconfirming to myself every day that this outcome is not only possible, but it also's inevitable, and secondly, to build upon that great moment. To absorb every single thing about that upcoming celebration and make it a part of who I am.

Once I've filled my entire being with that success, I then share my thanks with those who were involved in helping me achieve it. Gratitude is the attitude for all seasons of life, and in this case, it's one of the keys to your success. When you get fully associated into a state of gratitude, no negative emotion can survive in that atmosphere. It's much like diseases attempting to survive in an oxygen environment. It just doesn't happen.

Not only does gratitude feel great, but it also has a biochemical effect on your body in that it releases endorphins, which travel through every part of your body, filling you completely with that same feeling.

Imagine now how that feels. You've completed the task you set out to do, and your completely grateful for everyone, no matter how small or big of a part they played, and you have these incredible feel-good endorphins running frantically through your body! You feel more alive at this moment than you have in a long time. You can have this amazing experience every single day – all you have to do is develop the discipline to practice this over and over until it becomes second nature, or, in other words, do it over and over until it sticks!

In my own coaching practice, UE Coaching, my wife Steffany and I have teamed up to bring two incredibly important aspects together. Myself, being an Internationally Licensed Neuro-Linguistic Programming ("NLP") Master Practitioner and Certified Professional Coach, I enjoy working on discovering the mental roadblocks and limiting beliefs that many people experience, and then utilize individualized strategies to breakthrough and destroy them. Steffany is a Natural Health Practitioner who is also a Certified Clinical Iridologist and a Certified Professional Coach. Her passion is to focus on people's health, enabling them to break free of the health problems that have been holding so many people back for so long.

Steffany and I have found that by utilizing both of these modalities in tandem is especially effective in manifesting the change people desire, both mentally and physically.

How does this fit into discipline you ask? Let me share with you one of the phenomena, that, when mixed with just a small amount of discipline, can be all but eliminated.

Steffany works with her clients to first identify the symptoms of what they may be feeling and then digs deeper to find the root cause. Most of the times, through proper diet and the use of supplements she can have the client begin to notice improvements in their health in a relatively short period.

So, what do you think happens when most people start to feel better? Well, most people begin to cheat. A little extra snack here, maybe a donut there, and pretty soon they're back to where they were. She sees them again in three months, and they promptly let her know that the program isn't working. When she digs deeper and questions them on how much discipline and self-control they had with respect to sticking to the program, the truth comes out. It's at that point, when they recognized that they've all but lost the last three months, and need to start all over again, that they finally gain enough leverage on themselves to discover the discipline they require, to be able to stick with the program.

You see, discipline is critical not only for your mindset but also for the health of your body. Exercise is one thing that a lot of people will do anything to avoid. It's because they've linked up so much pain with the act of exercising that they would do almost anything, and tell themselves whatever they needed to, to get out of "getting physical."

If your goal or outcome is to lose twenty or thirty pounds, then it's imperative to understand that without a commitment to yourself, and the discipline to carry through on that commitment, you will most likely continue to gain weight, rather than to lose it. That's right...continue to GAIN weight because that's what you've been doing this whole time. You most likely didn't wake up and say wow...yesterday I was one hundred and sixty-five pounds, and now I'm two hundred and twenty pounds! No! This took time to happen, and you became very skilled at making happen. You found a pattern that enabled you to get to this weight without having to even think about it. It became a pattern, that, regardless if you want to hear it or not, you became very disciplined at. You're getting growth all right, unfortunately, its growth in the wrong kind of way, and it will certainly continue unless the pattern is interrupted and replaced with a much more empowering alternative.

Think about it like this. How easy is it to change the direction of a river? It takes a lot of work and planning to re-route that river to a new path, especially since it's been flowing in that same place for so long. It's carved out its exact path over centuries – a path that it now knows very well.

When constructions crews begin building dams in order to change the path of the river, they need to do it methodically and carefully, so that no part of the dam breaks and the river goes back to the way it was flowing. They need to continually ensure the integrity of the structure they are building so that there is no way the river can breach the new dam and go back to the way it used to be.

Once the river has been fully diverted, they need to ensure that the river keeps flowing in the new direction, until it becomes the new natural path of the river, until the river knows no other path than the new one that it's now on. All that work and all that discipline ensure that the outcome of the task is successful and there are no disasters along the way.

Isn't every success in life just like this? You plan out the outcome and then, utilizing discipline every step of the way, you ensure that you stay on the new path that you've set for yourself. Doesn't success require that you take a new path, and vehemently stick to it, to achieve your desired outcome? Have you ever seen anyone achieve success by doing the exact same thing over and over, making all the exact same mistakes, and then one day magically experience success? I highly doubt that anyone ever has! Have you ever heard the saying, that to do the same thing over and over, yet to expect a different result is the definition of insanity? Truer words could not have been spoken.

Thinking back to my own experience of being the contractor/employee, and recognizing that even after I had returned from UPW and knew that I was going to give notice, I continued to have those moments of "what if?" What if I wasn't successful on my own? What if things didn't work out and I had to come groveling back?

Now you might be saying, "I thought you had made the definitive decision that you were no longer going to accept the situation you were in?" To answer that question, YES, I did make that decision; however, those disempowering thoughts continued to test my own level of disciple and did whatever they could to step in whenever they could. And yes, sometimes I gave them just enough time to sink a small hook into me and draw me closer... to get me to think that maybe it's not so bad. That maybe I could push through this time because that constant paycheck gave me so much certainty.

But wait... how well did that work out for me last time I sacrificed what I knew to be true? How much satisfaction did I have in my life in those moments when I put what I knew was right, on the back burner?

Those questions gave me the pause I required. A pause long enough to ask an even better question: How can

I serve the people I plan to serve if I'm too busy doing someone else's work?

That was it. That was the silver bullet to kill the werewolf, better known as self-doubt, and get me back onto the path I knew was right.

You see, it was these moments that tested me, that enabled me to build on the level of discipline that I had. Remember how life is always happening for us? Life was certainly happening for me at this point because I figured out the valuable lesson it had to teach me. I learned that to have the outcome that I wanted; I had to be on my game continuously. Everyday I had to focus on exactly what it is that I would achieve once I succeeded, what it would mean to me and what it would mean to others once I had achieved success. Are disempowering thoughts going to come up? Sure they will, but are you going to let them control you, or instead, will you control them by telling them exactly where to go and how to get there?

It was a very similar level of discipline that enabled me to survive my divorce and custody challenge. At first, I did what I'm sure almost every parent who goes through a situation like this does: they go and get a lawyer. Initially, it felt good because here I was with this professional who knew all about this type of stuff, stuff that I really didn't know anything about. We began making headway, and my level of certainty increased as I saw progress. Things continued to go great until suddenly, the direction that I wanted to take, no longer became the direction my lawyer was taking. Now, I have to admit; I MUST be a slow learner because I did this same thing over and over with another three lawyers! Talk about not getting it the first, second or even third time! In total, it took me over five lawyers, and four years to finally figure it out - I was giving away my own voice, my own personal power, and allowing fear to control my actions. I had not developed the level of discipline required to be able to trust that I already had the answers within me.

Recognizing that my fear and lack of discipline was exactly what was preventing me from stepping into my own personal power, the fear of making the choice that I knew needed to be made. I asked myself a question: With all the skills that I had now learned, how much further ahead would I be if I stepped up and did what I knew within my heart needed to be done? What would happen if I now took responsibility and control of my destiny? It was at that moment at that time, that I switched from being outwardly focused - looking for someone to lead me and have them do what I believed I couldn't, to look inside, at all the amazing skills that I did have and how much further ahead I would be if I just stepped up.

Now I recognize this is a pretty extreme example - representing one's self, especially in such a high-profile way, can be a daunting task, however coming at it from a position of certainty in one's self can and will have a significant impact on the outcome. For me, I came to the realization that it was time - time for me to do what I knew I had to. It was time for me to dig into the incredible amount of knowledge that I had amassed and finally tap into it. It was time for fear to take a back seat. At that moment, I knew with certainty that I had taken my fate into my own hands, rather than leaving it to chance with someone else. I was filled with certainty in knowing that from this moment forward I was the one calling the shots and no matter what, the message that I carried within me would be the one delivered. In that moment of decision, my destiny was set.

I'm so incredibly happy to say that from that one decision I noticed a monumental increase in velocity with respect to the court proceedings. By me taking back my power and owning it, and developing the right level of discipline to stick to the path that I knew was right for me, and finally seeing myself for who and what I truly was, I radically changed the direction of the entire proceedings and finalized them all within one month of taking over.

This is the power, the true power of discipline. Find your cause, find your leverage and then practice over and over the exact steps, you will take to achieve your outcome, because with practice comes mastery.

To consistently achieve your desired outcome, whatever that may be, takes a certain discipline. A disciple that says every morning you will awaken and prime your body for an exceptional day. A disciple that says every day you will recognize those who have assisted you on your journey. Disciple means getting physically active at least five out of every seven days. Discipline means that nothing ever sends you on a detour that brings you further away from your goal.

Here's the best part. Once you make discipline a part of your life it first becomes a habit and then, the more you practice it, it turns into an addiction. It becomes something that you can no longer do without. It becomes who you are, and when you shape your life around who you label yourself as (I am an athlete, I am a runner, I am a healer), it becomes an inseparable part of your identity. Think of a person who used to smoke cigarettes. If after five years of not smoking you offered them a cigarette, would they say "no thank you, I used to be a smoker," or would they instead say, "no thank you, I'm not a smoker"? I would have to say that in most every case, that person would respond with the latter, because they utilized discipline on their journey to quit smoking, and as a part of that, they redefined who they are. The addiction to smoke turned into an addiction to become healthy.

Within the last couple of months, Steffany and I have taken up bike riding. We struggled for the longest time to discover a physical activity that we both enjoyed doing, and that we could do together. I myself enjoy running, and Steffany enjoys the stair climber at the gym. Yes, I could join her at the gym on that stair climber, but I'm sure I'd die of boredom looking at that same tan colored wall for forty-five minutes every day! The bottom line is, is that we both wanted to increase our physical health and get into better shape, and to do it, where we could both motivate each other, we landed on bicycle riding. I used to be quite active in the mountain biking scene. I never raced or anything of the sort, but would frequently ride the trails on the local ski hills in the summer. I really enjoyed it because it got my blood pumping, my adrenaline flowing and there was always new scenery passing me by.

Steffany was uncertain about riding at first, and I think she did it just to make me happy. For me, to ride on the local roadways was a bit boring, but we had finally found something we could do together. We didn't go out a lot at first because we hadn't built that discipline within each of us. We could always find the reasons why we wouldn't get out that day, either it was too cold, or we had to load the bikes onto the vehicle so that we could get to where we needed to be to ride, and that was too much work, and on and on. You see, we had no discipline to make this activity a must. It was a casual activity that we really had to plan to do.

As you can imagine, with a whole list of reasons (excuses) as to why we couldn't get out that day, or the next, or the next, we found it very easy to put off riding. Fortunately for us, our desire to reshape our bodies, into something other than round, was all the leverage we needed. Instead of worrying about packing the bikes up to go somewhere to ride, we made a choice to ride right from our home. This took one heck of a commitment and a whole lot of discipline from us because we live at the top of a hill. Starting out the ride is great because it's all downhill... it's that four kilometers back up the hill that nearly did us in the first few times!

We persevered, and the hill became easier and easier. Now I'd be lying to you if I told you it's now a piece of cake. It still works up a good heart rate and makes me sweat, but the difference now is that we crave it. The challenge of seeing if we can make an even better time, every time we ride, has evolved from needing the discipline to stick to it, to becoming an addiction that we almost can't do without. Any day that we don't ride, we feel the draw and call of it. To not ride now brings us much more pain than the initial hesitation we felt when we first began riding.

When you're open to welcoming discipline into your life, your life begins to change rapidly. If you're committed to making the changes in your life that you know you need to, and if you're ready to step into your new life today, then say YES!

PUTTING IT ALL TOGETHER

CHAPTER 7 - PUTTING IT ALL TOGETHER

Congratulations! This is the part where you celebrate! Yes, that's right, celebrate! Take this moment to recognize that you've come a long way from where you were when you first picked up this book. Maybe you were curious about the cover, or maybe you wondered if it could actually get you onto the path you've always know that you were meant to be on. Maybe you're at that point where you know that change is an absolute must in your life and that you're prepared to do whatever it takes! Whatever the reason, I sincerely congratulate you for taking this giant step towards transforming your life.

It's a statistical fact that only ten percent of people make it past the first chapter, and for you, to be here, so close to the end is incredibly exciting! And with some of the most exciting, most juicy bits to come, it's no wonder why you're reading these words as fast as you are.

We've covered some great concepts so far, and to take it one step further I'd like to combine it all into a scenario. I'd like to show you how applying each of these four individual dimensions can empower you to achieve success in your life starting *today!*

Now, this next scenario is only one possible use of the four dimensions, however, you can take each of the dimensions and apply them to your specific situation. It could be how to attract the perfect partner into your life, or it could be about doubling your total business over the next year. Whatever your desired outcome, by simply applying these principles you can have exactly what it is you desire.

That's the beauty of this. It's like a universal translator. No matter the outcome or what language is being spoken, anyone can take this simple principle and put it to work for them to get their exact outcome.

One of my clients, who recently started working with me, came to be coached on how to take charge of his health. This client, who at one time had played semi-professional sports, was now no longer in that peak state of health (Remember earlier on when I made a comment about round being a shape as well? That applies to this exact situation!). He found himself putting on more weight than he was comfortable with and was really noticing that it wasn't coming off as easy as it once had. In fact, it was no longer coming off at all.

Unlike most first sessions I wanted to try something different with him. Before we got going, I let him know that the only way I could work with him is that he must do everything I told him. I let him know that I was also working on a new process that would guarantee his outcome; however, the process only worked for those who were the absolutely most committed. That without that ultimate level of commitment he may as well take what he was about to pay me and burn it.

Another thing about my practice; I charge a lot for people to work with me. I don't do it because I'm greedy, and I don't do it because I'm looking to make a quick buck, I do it to create the level of commitment required to facilitate change. What that means, is if you pay someone forty dollars for an hour of coaching and you get nothing out of it, oh well, it's only forty dollars. However, if you pay between five hundred to one thousand dollars per hour, I can guarantee you that you will take whatever steps you need to see that you get every ounce of value out of what I share. This monetary value has the greatest motivating value within people, and I've seen it consistently work over and over.

My client profusely let me know that he was completely committed and that he would do whatever I said. I then let him know that I was going to place a twenty-five-hundred-dollar charge on his credit card. I explained to him that if he was truly committed like he said he was, then there would be no risk to him, because at the end when he had achieved his goal, he would be refunded this money. However, if he missed appointments and didn't follow through on taking the steps to achieving the outcomes and goals that he set, he would forfeit the money.

This was a little bit of a hard pill for him to swallow. I told him that I understood that he might not have the commitment required, because this program was truly for those who wanted to achieve their outcome, not for those who only hoped to have success. That this program certainly wasn't for everybody, and that I really understood if he wasn't ready to make the changes that only true champions were ready for (remember the semi-pro athlete part here).

That did it. Within seconds I had his card in my hand, and I processed the twenty-five-hundred-dollar charge. This is the level of commitment I was looking for. When someone is not afraid to step up and be completely willing to do whatever it takes to achieve their goal, you know that they have stepped into that special state of being unstoppable.

Next, we started out with the outcome. I asked him what success looked like for him, and what it represented to him. He began with the usual answers like "I'd feel better," "My clothes would fit me." I stopped him right there and said "no... what does success *really* look like for you?".

Prior to meeting my clients for the first time, I have them complete a questionnaire that digs into what's most important to them. I knew that my client valued family, especially his children, and I wanted him to make the connection between his ultimate outcome, and exactly how it related to his children. To make that connection and to link up how that success involved them, was going to be one of my key strategies to get him to the finish line.

He was confused at first until I had him close his eyes and then walked him through a visualization exercise. The exercise was a bit longer than most, however, when that connection was made, you could see his complete physiology change. He became so much more certain in achieving that goal, even more confident than when I charged the twenty-five-hundred-dollars onto his card!

We had defined the outcome, and that was being fit and healthy so that he could be there for his kids as they grew into adults themselves. The goal was no longer just about him, it had grown to include those he valued the most, and because of that, his level of commitment increased exponentially. He could now see himself at his children's graduation, at their weddings and at the birth of his first grandchild. He could now clearly see the outcome, along with exactly what that outcome meant to him.

Now attached to every successful outcome there must be a completion date, and in my client's case, I also wanted to understand what his specific target was with respect to an exact weightless amount. At first, he had difficulty identifying a specific date on which he would have achieved his goal. I'm sure that no part of that hesitation linked to him calculating how quick he could do it before he forfeited the twenty-five-hundred-dollars I had just charged him!

I had him walk through another quick visualization exercise (which we cover in the goal setting workshop) and he had the date! You see, there was far too much chatter going on in his head. Too many voices saying "if you pick this date, you may not have enough time." When you can shut those voices off, you allow the truth to speak.

Next was the total weight loss. I asked him "How much weight would you need to lose, or what would be your perfect weight now that you have achieved success?".

There wasn't as much hesitation coming up with this number, and I know a lot of that had to do with him already having seen and experienced that outcome.

There it was! He had defined success! He saw the outcome and felt the result of it. He knew the exact moment when he had achieved that success, and he knew the total amount of weight he already lost! Most importantly he knew exactly why he was doing it.

I felt lucky at this very moment because I had achieved a two for one. I was able to discover exactly what success looked like for my client, PLUS I was able to define the cornerstone for the first dimension. I had his desire. All we had to do was expand it to epic proportions.

I found this to be probably the easiest of the four dimensions because there was so much leverage to be used. I discussed with him what it will mean to him, to have reached his goal and how he would interact with his children differently. You see, he had shared with me that there were things he *wanted* to do with his children, however, because it had been so long since he had, and because of the amount of weight he gained, he felt embarrassed even to try. Riding his bicycle was one of those things. Even though he had recently purchased the children new bikes, they had never yet ridden with Dad, because let's face it, dad was FAT!

Identifying his exact situation as being not just a little heavy, or as having put on a few pounds, but that he was fat, added to his desire. To get the ultimate outcome that a person desires, it's critically important to really understand where they are right now, and where they want to be. Had we stuck with the idea that my client was "slightly overweight," or "had a few extra pounds," it wouldn't provide the same level of leverage in getting him to understand the severity of the situation. That he was fat, and if he did nothing about it, he'd miss out on so much of his children's future. When I asked him how he felt when he was an athlete vs. how he felt now, I could see him physically cringe. We discussed that moment when he was in that peak state and then brought that forward by asking him how things would be different with the children now if he was still at that level of physical fitness.

We continued this discussion till I felt that the desire was firmly planted and that he had not just one, but multiple reasons to reflect back on, in case he felt he could "just this one time" let things slide.

Next came determination.

Because my client was a former semi-pro athlete, it was easy for me to work on the determination aspect. I had him go back in his mind to when he was just young, out on that hockey rink all alone at five am in the morning, practicing shooting pucks at the net. I asked him why he did it and he explained to me that he had a dream to go as far as he could with hockey. I challenged him and said "well... most of us have dreams every night, what's different about that dream?". "No, no, not that kind of dream," he said, "It's the kind of dream where you think about it all the time, and you do whatever it takes to make it come to life. The kind of dream that you have over and over, and even when you're awake you can see it."

I smiled because I knew that this would work perfectly. I asked him about when he first had the dream and why, and he told me it was because it was something he and his father watched a lot of growing up. It was their time together watching hockey that helped to create the incredible bond that they had, and it's what got his interest piqued at a very young age. He also found out very quickly that it was something he was naturally good at.

I asked him what would happen if he didn't go to practice and he looked back at me with a funny look. "What do you mean not go to practice?" He asked. "There was no such thing as not going to practice, and even if I did want to skip out on practice, my dad would come in and haul my ass out of bed and tell me to get my gear on!"

This gave me another huge clue for the accountability portion of my coaching, and I made a note of that because seeing that when he had no other choice, regardless of if he wanted to or not, he had the dedication to get it done.

To bring this same level of dedication forward, I made the relationship between him and his father relative to that of him and his kids. Out doing physical activities, riding those bikes and having those same moments of bonding and connection, just like he had with his own father. Make no mistake; I did employ a bit of pain to the current situation, reminding him that he could never have that same relationship with his own children as he had with his father if he were to do nothing and remain on the same path that he had been on until this point. I let him know that if it couldn't be him coaching his children because he had moved from fat to obese, then it would have to be some other man, some other coach that would have to stand in as their mentor. Someone who they could look up to. Someone who would help them create their very own dreams and aspirations for their lives.

You want to talk about going from zero to one hundred! I had him. There was no way some other guy would come along and coach his children, or be their mentor when he was perfectly capable! That was the leverage I needed to get him to commit fully, to get him to a level of commitment to determination of one hundred on a scale that only goes to ten.

Next came dedication. What was going to keep him on this path? I chose to use more pain for this.

Now you might think I'm some sort of masochist causing all my clients so much pain, but that's not it at all. You see, as humans, we have two primary motivating factors and those are to either seek pleasure or avoid pain. Because I had already linked up a lot of pleasure with seeing the outcome for exactly what my client wanted, it was time for him to see what he didn't want.

I asked him several very critical questions, and those questions were, what does your life look like, first in six months and then in one year and then in three years if you do absolutely nothing different than what you're doing now? How will your life be if you keep going to the Pizza Hut all you can eat buffet and are double and triple stuffing yourself on all the desserts that they have, *after* you've already filled up on the thousands of calories you had from the pizza you just finished devouring?

Because I wanted details, lots of them, I had him again describe this to me through a closed eye exercise. I had him go deep into exactly what it would mean to huff and puff and feel that chest pain every time he walked up the steps into his house, not knowing if he was going to make it, or if instead, he would fall down clenching his chest because of how badly clogged up his arteries were.

I used this particular example as in his original questionnaire he had indicated that at times he did feel pain in his chest and that even the simple task of walking up one flight of stairs would cause him to breathe heavily and even start to break out into a light sweat.

I then asked him what it would feel like to go to a reunion of all his old hockey buddies. What would they think of him? Would they still see him as the young star that he once was, or would they instead see him as the fat water boy?

I continued on, having him describe in detail what it would be like going to his kid's graduation, being one of the largest dads in the crowd, and how his kids would feel about having a dad that had to carefully select the right chair to sit on for fear of breaking it due to his weight.

I then took him even further into the future, having him see himself being who he would be if nothing changed. I asked him to describe to me how he felt. His answer: Alone. When I questioned him about why he was alone, he told me that because of who he had become (I think he may have made a reference to Jabba the Hut at this point), nobody wanted to have him around. He was alone because of the choices he made and because of the choices he didn't make. He was embarrassed about his size and didn't want anyone that he used to know, see him looking like this.

It was when I asked him about his children that he became silent. This was it. This was his point of no more, and it was unmistakable.

Because he knew with complete certainty that if he didn't make the changes that needed to be made, the changes that must be made, he would lose what meant the most to him, and that was not an acceptable outcome. That negative outcome would never do because it was not the future that he saw.

We finished the closed eye exercise and then reflected for a few minutes on what he experienced. He discovered that even though for the time being, the negative outcome he saw was a worst-case scenario, if he did nothing and decided not to dedicate his time and effort to obtain the successful outcome he saw, then that worst case outcome *would become* his future. He recognized that he must reorganize his life and restructure his priorities so that the only outcome would be the successful one.

This took us to discipline. Things in my client's life had to change, and they had to change big time. There could be no half-assing it, no cheating on Sundays and certainly no making excuses as to why he couldn't get his butt up off the couch. He had to start somewhere, and as a part of his commitment to the program, I had him tell me where he would begin. He was committed to starting by going for a walk at least once in the morning and once at night - every morning and every night.

Together we developed a healthy eating list. With this list, if there was something in his house that wasn't on the list then it either went in the garbage or sent to the local food bank if it wasn't opened.

To ensure that he completed this task, I reminded him that if he did not, he would forfeit the twenty-five-hundred-dollars that he had given me, PLUS I would be popping by one random day to ensure that he did what he said he was going to. Now I don't do this for every one of my clients but remember for this client; he worked best when he had no other option other than to make the change. This little piece of added accountability ensured that he would achieve his outcome.

Together we also developed a well-balanced meal plan that would eliminate the "all you can eat" Pizza Hut lunches. Gone were the days of lunches and dinners that were way too many calories to count. We came up with ideas for healthy dinners that he could then bring the next day for lunch.

Next was coming up with an exercise regime. We decided that he would start with walking twice a day, every day, once in the morning and once at night, for at least forty-five minutes, and that our next coaching session would be done on his walk, that way he could be doubly effective at ensuring his outcome was achieved, while at the same time, not providing any reasons for not going out for the walk (I couldn't walk today because I had the coaching session with you). Once he was comfortable with the walk, we would transition to the local gym and then finally onto riding the bike that he had committed to purchasing.

That was the ticket. That was the secret sauce for my client to take the steps he needed to begin the transformation in his life. I'm happy to say that this client did indeed go on to achieve the goal he set out to, and as a matter of fact, he was able to complete the goal *before* the timeline that he had set out for himself.

Because I'm a curious kind of guy, I asked him if it was hard to do what he set out to do. He let me know that at first there were challenges. Going through his house and getting rid of all the food that he loved was a tough one to do; however, the opposite side of the coin was *even tougher. Not* taking the steps created even more pain for him and because of this, he got the task done that very first night after his coaching session.

Exercising wasn't as hard as he thought it would be because even though it had been a long time since he seriously strapped on his skates, he remembered what it felt like to be in that peak physical state, and that drove him to want to feel that way again. Even though we had set a deadline for the gym membership at one month after he started his program, within two weeks, he was at the gym beginning his workouts, first thing in the morning, before he got his day started.

When I asked him what the most important factor was for staying on the path that he had started, he let me know that it was the future that he saw every single morning when he woke up, and how grateful he was for having a program like this that ensured he would be there for his children as they grew older. He had incorporated the visioning and gratitude exercise into his morning ritual, and any day that he missed it, he knew that he felt incomplete.

I also asked him if he felt like cheating or giving up and he said there were times; however, it was always the thought of his children that kept him going and never giving up.

Oh, and by the way, he did get his twenty-five-hundred-dollars back, and he used it to buy a brand-new mountain bike so he could enjoy that time with his kids.

The principle of these four dimensions can be used for any desired outcome, and I'm happy to offer it both in person at our live seminars and through our online webinars. These core principles can be used not only in your personal life but also in businesses of all sizes from small to multinational corporations. By creating and designing your perfect outcome and then following through with each of the four dimensions, you too can be the unstoppable force that you know you're destined to be.

For more information on this book or to discover how to reserve your spot for our next live or web seminar, please contact either myself or Neil at info@uecoaching.com or info@shindao.com. After you've attended this transformational training, your life will never be the same!

If all this training did was to help you get crystal clear on your goals, and help you to achieve them like never before, would it be worth it? Only you can answer that question!

THE BONUS MATERIAL

CHAPTER 8 - THE BONUS MATERIAL

In everyone's life there is always at least one or two "Ah Ha!" moments. If you've not had that moment, get a hold of me right now and let's get you your breakthrough today! Seriously though, these are those life defining moments. Moments when it all clicks together and everything becomes clear. My moment happened for me when I discovered the main reason why I did the things I did, and why, for the most part, I made the decisions I do.

It sounds like a pretty lofty claim to totally understand why you do the things you do, doesn't it?

The best part is, is that it's completely true.

My breakthrough happened several years ago when I first listened to a little cd program called The Ultimate Edge, by Tony Robbins. Now if you haven't figured it out yet, I'm a pretty big Tony Fan. I guess you would say I'm one of those Raving Fans that he talks about all the time. NO, it's not because I love to drop names and pretend that I'm associated with all these big-name people, it's because what he shared in that program made such a massive impact in my life.

You see, in that program set, I was introduced to the Six Human Needs, or as some people refer to it, the Psychology of the Six Human Needs.

Why was it such a big deal to me? Because it made sense! Here I was all my life wondering why I would make one decision over another, why I would choose to always wait for the walk sign before crossing the road. Why I used to always need to be seen and recognized for the work I had done.

So, what are the Six Human Needs?

- Certainty
- Uncertainty
- Significance
- Love and Connection
- Growth
- Contribution

Let me run through an exercise with you, to help you discover where you stand right now, and what needs you value the most. Remember… these are NEEDS. They are not "nice to have's" nor are they simply passing feelings. These are the actual needs of your soul and spirit. They are the driving force that defines why you do the things you do.

To begin this exercise, draw a large circle on a piece of paper. Now once you have the circle, I'd like you to draw six spokes, equidistant apart. Now on each of those spokes, I'd like you to draw four small intersecting lines, again the distance between each of those lines should be roughly equal. You'll now have a circle (or a pie if you prefer) with six equal pie-shaped sections.

Starting with the section closest to the eleven o'clock position I'd like you to begin naming each section of the pie, first with certainty, then uncertainty then significance, then love and connection, then growth and finally contribution. Once completed, your diagram should look like the one pictured below.

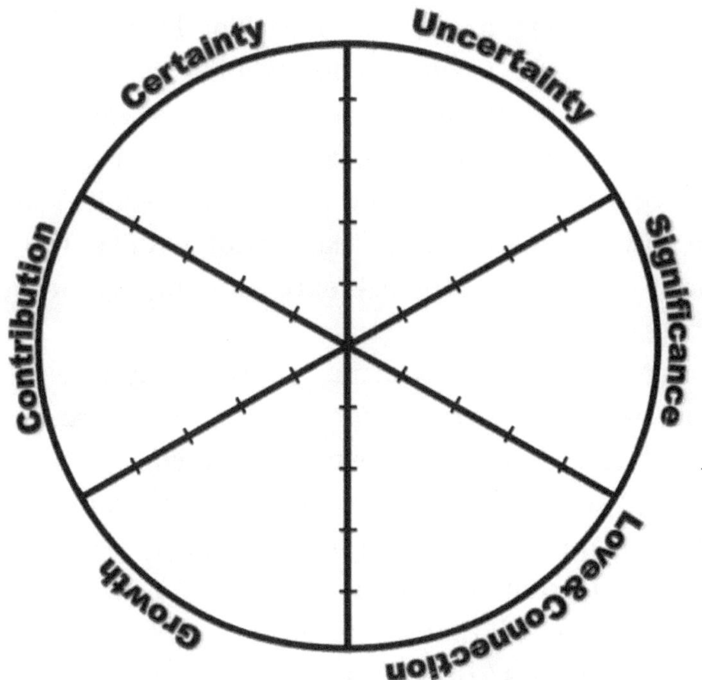

Let's start with Certainty. So, what is certainty, and what does it mean to you? Many people have different meanings of what certainty means to them. For some people, it's knowing that they'll always have their partner there for them, no matter what the situation. Being certain to others may mean that they need to know beyond a shadow of a doubt that they have their budget laid out for the next three months. It can also mean knowing for sure where they're going to lay their head tonight. Certainty for many, is security, knowing that what they have planned for is exactly how things will turn out.

How much does certainty play a role in your life and how important, on a scale of one to ten, is it for you?

In each piece of the pie, you have those four small lines intersecting the sections of each of the pieces - these are in increments of two. So, for example, if your current level of certainty in your life right now is six, you'd draw a line from the third small line, across the certainty section, to the other third small line on the opposite side. You can then go ahead and shade in that section with your pen or pencil to give you a graphical representation of your rating of that specific need.

Moving on to Uncertainty now, many of you like surprises? Like a birthday surprise, or winning an exotic tropical trip, or coming home to find that your partner has surprised you with a fantastic dinner? I know for me, it's a real treat to find something new and exciting in my life. Doesn't uncertainty feel great? Well, how about that unexpected tax bill that you forgot to save for and is now due in two weeks? How about coming home and finding out that you had left the garage door open all day, and strangely enough, the garage looks a little more bare than usual? Uncertainty comes in many forms; however, the quality of your life is directly related to the amount of uncertainty you can handle.

Going back to imagining you won that exotic tropical trip, how do you feel? My hallucination is that you have a whole lot of excitement coursing through your body because it's new, it's something you may not have done before, and it brings you uncertainty in a really great way.

Imagine that same trip now, and imagine that you knew exactly how every second and every moment of that trip would be, knowing in advance exactly who you'll see and meet, what you'll have every day for dinner, and exactly how that will taste! Yes, you've got a whole lot of certainty there with knowing exactly how everything is going to be; however, the excitement is lost! Uncertainty brings us that, both in positive and sometimes not so positive forms. How would you rate your level of comfort with uncertainty? Do you have a whole lot of it in your life now, welcoming it with open arms, or would you rather have a handle on things, preferring to be more in control? Go ahead and rate your level of comfort with uncertainty now.

Moving on to Significance, which is how important it is for you be seen and heard, for what and who you are, how do you see this need ranking in your life? Is it important to you as a boss or a supervisor to have your direct reports see you as a leader, as the person in charge? Do you feel that you offer a contribution to the social, mental or economic well-being of those in your life? Significance in this aspect is related to the level of importance you associate yourself with others. In other words, do you feel that you play a meaningful role in someone's life whereby if you weren't there to fulfill that person's need, they would suffer without you? How important to you is it that people see you as someone that they come to because you are the one that has the ability to give them what they require? Perhaps your significance is obtained from meeting the needs of your children, you being their day to day provider. As before, rate yourself on your current level of significance to others.

Love and Connection can best be described as how well you feel connected to yourself and those that are close to you. Do you find that you stay connected to the people you care about often and share with them how special they are and how much you love them? Do they do this for you? Do you have a passion in your life that stimulates you to appreciate life on a higher level? Do you show affection with those you care about by holding hands, giving a hug or even a gentle touch? In this section, you're going to rate exactly how big of a role love and affection play in your life. Go ahead and rate the current level of connection in your life right now.

All things in nature must either grow or die...there is no in between. Do you feel that you're growing in all areas of your life now? Are those that are in your life growing with you or are they instead growing apart from you? Are you willing to learn the tools and put forth the energy to make massive changes in your life? Do you constantly seek out new opportunities that motivate you to see the world in a new light, with a new greater purpose?

Growth is essential in your life, and to have a successful and fulfilling life, you must always be growing. Growth contributes to many of your other needs, such as uncertainty, in that growth brings newness to your life.

Growth also contributes to significance, because as you advance in both your life and career, isn't it true that you naturally become more significant? Where is your life right now, with respect to the level of growth you are experiencing? Do you find that there is plenty of growth with everything you have right now, or do you feel that you have reached a point of stagnation, a plateau, that requires a good shake-up to restart your forward momentum? Rate your current level of growth right now in the growth section of the circle.

Lastly, but certainly not least is Contribution. Contribution provides each of us a sense of service and focuses on helping, giving and supporting others. Contribution is a spiritual need that provides the most fulfillment of any of the six needs. Stop for a moment and think of how good it feels to contribute in life. How does it make you feel when someone does something completely selfless for you, meaning that they do it out of love and caring with no expectation of reciprocation? What is your current level of contribution in your life right now? Do you contribute to others through donations, volunteering and food drives? Where do you make your biggest contributions in life? Go ahead and rate your current level of contribution to others now.

Congratulations! You have now completed your personal evaluation of the six human needs! How balanced are you in your results? If you pictured your circle as a wheel on a bicycle, what type of ride would it give you? Would it be a nice smooth ride, or would it instead be a bumpy one? How does this compare to where you thought you would be before starting this exercise? Are there areas where you are congruent with what you knew to be true? Do you also see areas where there are differences in what you perceived life is or "should" be? If you've identified areas that need more balance in your life, I'd like to congratulate you AGAIN, as you now have a clear path as to exactly what areas to focus in on your life right now!

Because you now have this amazing graphical representation, I'd like you to take a moment to make a few notes of exactly which top two needs require the most work, and what steps you could take right now, to immediately begin filling those areas in your life. Put the book down for just a moment and write down what you could do, or what you will do, right now to work on those needs.

So, what did you come up with for actionable items? Is there something you can do right now, or after you finish reading this section, that will drive you forward to getting the work done that you've identified? By taking massive, determined action right at the very moment you define that action is required, almost always ensures that you will accomplish whatever it is you've set out to do.

Conversely, for those who fail to take action, rarely do they ever see their desired outcome, and even more rarely do they have the opportunity to celebrate the fruit of their labors.

Remember, it doesn't have to be something big. Sometimes the smallest actions can have the most profound impact.

What change could you make right now, that will have an impact today? What change are you prepared to make that will transform your life right *NOW*?

This is the exercise that changed my life the most. I recognized very quickly that at a time, my two top needs were certainty and significance, and I lived a life that was congruent to having these needs consistently met! How exciting of a life do you think I led when I wouldn't even cross the road without having the "walk now" sign lit up – even though there were no cars for miles?! I recognized that if I wanted to start living – to *truly start living*, I had to rebalance my needs.

Remember my old question: What's my purpose? When I refocused on contribution, one of my lowest ranked needs at the time, and changed it from being the least important to the most important, my question was finally answered. Because of that, I was able to develop my new empowering question: How can I help even more people live a life that is free from unnecessary suffering NOW? This new question changed everything about who I am. Not only that, because I had significantly rearranged the order of my needs, having Contribution, Growth and Love and Connection as my top three needs, I became someone else. Someone whose values looked absolutely nothing like the person I once was, and someone who is truly driven to improve the lives of everyone that I have the pleasure of meeting. It took me practicing every one of the four dimensions every day, for me to become the person I am now.

It's those principles, those specific dimensions, when followed with unwavering passion and commitment, that will provide you with *all* the fruits in life. Take these principles right now and begin your amazing new journey of success on your terms.

Here's one last bit of secret sauce – once I began making changes, my entire life began transforming almost immediately! Yes… it was that quick. Change happens in an instant. All you have to do is welcome it into your life. Be accepting of change, because if you think you can't change, you won't, but if you think you can change, and you know with certainty that change and success are your only option, then hold on, because you're about to experience one incredible ride.

AUTHORS NOTE

This book is only the beginning of the incredible journey of transformation that you are about to embark on, and for that I am excited! I want to thank you for being part of my own personal evolution, and for allowing me to share my journey thus far with you.

I learned a great many lessons through some of the most difficult times in my life, and if I can help even one person avoid that same pain, then I can rest easy knowing that I accomplished what I set out to do. That was the true purpose of this book – to share a story of hope, a story of inspiration. To let everyone know that they have the ability within them to take charge of their lives and manifest the future they've always wanted.

The secret to success for me is four parts dimensional and one-part mindset. I have to be in the space of complete expectation of the success, knowing with certainty that success really is the only option, and that failure would be akin to death. I must see how my success benefits the greater good, (improving others by helping them removing unnecessary suffering) and even if it is a class two experience to start with, I have all the Desire, Determination, Dedication and Discipline I need to ensure that the outcome I set, is the outcome I end up with, and that class two experience, becomes a class one experience.

Those were the exact steps I took when writing this book. I envisioned the day I would finally hold a copy of it in my hands, who would be there and what it would mean to me and how it will help others. That crystal-clear outcome, along with the complete expectation of accomplishment is what got me here, to this point now. It took me a while to really get into the flow of writing, but once I did, I became unstoppable. The more I worked on practicing Desire, Determination, Dedication, and Discipline, the better I got, and before I knew it, the words were flowing out of me faster than I could type. It was those very four dimensions, applying them and practicing them each and every day that ensured my success.

Take those very same ideals and principles and put them to work for you today. Dare yourself to break the mold and do something you've never done before. Set an outrageous tantalizing goal, something that is deeply meaningful to you, and go out and achieve it!

Becoming the change that you've always wanted to be is one hundred percent within your grasp because all it takes is the Desire, the Determination, the Dedication and the Discipline to make it happen. You are absolutely worth it!